The Basket

by Roger Blank

RoseDog Books

PITTSBURGH, PENNSYLVANIA 15238

RoseDog Books
585 Alpha Drive
Suite 103
Pittsburgh, PA 15238
Visit our website at *www.rosedogbookstore.com*

ISBN: 978-1-6442-6757-8
eISBN: 978-1-6442-6780-6

Every

story has to have a narrator, so I need to be it. I'm going to start with it's all crazy and hectic around here, tryin' to write and think at the same time. Well, I don't know what to say. All that's coming to my mind is it's all about the thinking to excite people who read or at least listen. Sometimes I don't read enough to listen what the words are sayin'. I probably don't make any sense, but they do if you read in between the lines. I will start to think now what to write as I go. Nuts, I forgot to say who I am. We can come to that in a bit. If I start telling what I'm writing about, then maybe you will get to know me and I will say my name. Let me think about it for a minute. My name is Jim Starling, and I have to tell you about a life of an interesting guy lost in his life, hoping to find his way. You got to hear this one, okay?

I looked into the mirror one day and asked where my life went. I got to start life again but still wondered, too. Today is another day. Why is it going to get better soon? I had a life once but I don't anymore. It was an interesting life for a person to have. I was twenty-five, it was fun when I let it be a good day. What's a good day? Well, let's see, not getting fired, not getting shot. Be your own person. Do what you want to do without hurting anyone or their feelings. I just hurt my own feelings and mind when I don't think right. I sometimes do the wrong planning and start something else and don't finish what I started to do in the first place. Just like this story, I tell you my age and say my name. I wasn't thinking about it. My mind travels fast. No, I didn't tell you my name yet. Well, here we go.

My name is Tom Buddy. I'm forty-five and I live anywhere I need to be. If something happens and it involves me, I say, "Stay there." Where is there? Well, it's where my mind tells me to go. It sounds scary and it is some days, but got to live it out for now. It will change again and again. Sounds screwed up, hey. Well, it's all there if you let go there. All I know is that you don't know what I'm going to say next. Me either, to make you feel better. It's the way my mind works. I think and say things different. I will tell the story right when I ever get there. I wear clothes that I find. The cleaner the garbage is, the better the clothes are. Garbage is not always garbage; people just call it that. I like to call it opportunity for the needed. If you need it, take it. I wear a hat. It's a kind of fancy one, it's a brownish gray one. People wear it when they are dressed up. Brim all the way around and folds in the center, not too high up. I also have a warm trench coat jacket, what people wear in the winter months. I found a scarf just the other day. My gloves are worn out but still keep me warm during this time. I have a pair of warm boots. The laces are getting worn out, but I'll find a pair of laces tomorrow. Maybe next week or month or year. It's okay, a pair will show up. I do wear socks but they got lots of holes in them. I will find a pair of them soon as I can find a pair. I live on the street and also in the woods. I like the woods but need to be prepared for the woods. I need a sleeping bag and maybe an old tent or at least a tarp. I can make a place out of branches, too. I do travel a lot when it's time to move on. I do. I get bored.

Yeah, you could say I'm homeless, but if you make a place of your own you're not. It might not be the biggest place, but I can call it my own. Park benches are okay for napping during the day, but it's only for a short nap. I don't worry; some people don't have a bench to sleep on. I found one one day, it had a bum leg but I fixed what I could and I can call it my own. People throw away the best stuff. I found an old wooden box that was the same height as the other leg on the bench and used it for a leg. That's where I sit and take naps. Where do I have it? Well, it's on a hill overviewing the city. I have a few trees around. Sunsets are nice and sunrises are very cool. I have a lean-to under the tree by the bench. It's beautiful up here. You would like it if you were here to see it. Lots of people don't see it 'cause they are too busy.

I decide to gather up some wood for a fire. I start a fire and it is very peaceful sitting on my bench, looking at the fire. I start to think about my past. I think of my childhood for a bit. It was not the best childhood, but it was not as bad as some of my friends'. My dad was an alcoholic and my mother was a whore. I have three brothers and a sister that I never have met. I was only fourteen when my sister was born, but I was not living with my parents at the time of her birth. I stayed with my aunt and uncle for the rest of my childhood years. My parents were into drugs also. They have both been busted for the drugs. It was a very screwed-up situation that I think about a lot. It's not easy to talk about. I don't like to think about it, but I need to get it out somehow. So I write about it a lot. I find some paper and a pencil that has been sharpened by a knife of mine many times over. It is a pencil that I found at a restaurant a year ago. I went in there to eat, someone gave me some money and I went to a restaurant and ate great food. A nice waitress gave me her pencil and I have kept it all this time. I write down what I want to say when things bother me. It helps me think.

The waitress I saw might have been my little sister, but I don't know. Like I said, I have not seen my sister before so I wouldn't know. I would love to meet her someday, but I don't know if I would want to yet. Maybe she wants to find me, but also at the same time maybe she doesn't want me to meet any of her family. I wouldn't know, I guess. It would be nice to know she's all right and taken care of by some good people. We were all split up when my parents were on drugs. So I don't even know if they are even around yet. Don't know and don't care right now. My brothers were good, but they did pick on me a lot. It would be good to see them again sometime. I don't know where they're at right now, but I could find them if I really want to.

I need a narrator moment right now. It's not easy to write about stuff that happens to people out there. I like the story that I'm telling, but it's tough to talk about it. My three cats are looking at me, wondering what I'm doing on a typewriter, and they are having a stare-down among each other. It's funny to watch them in action. Relaxing in ways, now I think I can write again about the story. Okay, now where was I? I was talking about finding my brothers, if I wanted to. Well, okay. On the next page I will talk about my brothers a bit.

I got a brother that is eight years older than me. I have another brother that is five years older than me and another brother that is three years older than me. I have a sister that I haven't met yet. She is at least ten years younger than me. Let's talk a little bit about my oldest brother. He was the oldest and ran the show all the time. What he always said went. Dad wasn't around much, so he would step up to the plate. He would work around the neighborhood for quick cash for us. You got to respect that he did that for us. We were hungry. He wasn't afraid to work. He would shove dog shit out of people's yards to keep it up, mow their lawns, trim their trees, paint their houses and garages, pave their driveways. He was fifteen years old when that was done. I was eight. His name was Darrel. I don't know what he is doing now or where he is at. When I went to live with my aunt and uncle, he went to live with grandparents in a different state. I think Florida, where it's 80 in December. My grandparents traveled a lot. So he went with them. Like I said, we split up to live with people when our parents were busted.

My other brother, he liked to fight a lot. His name was Randel, we called him Red for short. He would leave blood on the ground after hitting someone. It was as red as blood. I don't know if he ever became a boxer or not, but I could find out if I kept looking in the paper for him. It would be cool if he was, because he would be great. I would sneak in to watch him if he was boxing. I loved that brother of mine. When a few guys was picking on me when we were young, he put both of them in their place, a place of hurting. He's my bro. I have a third brother, he became a salesman. He sold furniture of some sort. He also sold cars. He sold vacuums, too. He had traveled around for that job. Sold what he could to live off of what he made. I haven't seen him in a while, but I heard he got married a few years ago and got a kid. I hope he is happy. He was the smart one of the family. He always wanted to be a family man. Good guy, maybe I will look him up someday. I like to travel, so maybe I can locate him. His name is Danniel. I hope to see him soon. Maybe he is only down the hill from here. Quick trip to town to find out if he is or not.

The fire is getting a low flame, so I need to get more wood. I like fires. I like the flame and warmth. I can chat more about my young life in a bit. Tomorrow is another day. I used to ride my bike a lot in my youth. I was good at it. Someday I will get another bike ride while the wind is at my back.

I find more wood and I will put more on the fire. I will have enough for the night. I will turn in for the night. I will go down the hill into town in the morning. I will look for food and maybe see if my brother Dan is around town. I lie down in my lean-to and I fall asleep.

The warm, bright sun wakes me up. The sound of traffic in the distance. I can see a lot of people driving cars and trucks. I need coffee. I used to drink coffee in the mornings. Maybe I can get a cup. Sometimes I wash people's windows on their cars. I usually wash them at the stoplight when they are stopped. I do it quick and they do like it, and I once in a while get a dollar for it. Then I will get my cup of coffee. I like this old café on the corner. It's a good café. It has a looka-like old boxcar. It's more like a caboose from the old days. It's red. Back in the day, they used red cabooses to indicate the end of the train. All the railroads had them. The café has an old boxcar and a caboose with it. Quick window wash and let's have a cup of joe.

I get ready to head down the hill to town. I have to cross a busy highway. It has six lanes, busy place. I look for cars, no cars, and I run across. I get across and down under the overpass. I see the street-lights, and I do have my favorite one I wash windows at. I will see my regular people drive by. When I see them, I will wash them first. They treat me okay. I wash this one guy's car window. He has an older car, looks like a 1966 Belvedere station wagon. It is light blue. He al-ways waves to me, and I grab my pail and squeegee and have a spray bottle that I fill up with water, and I have it lying behind a bench. It is next to the building, so I can hide it behind a wall if I need to.

I have my bottle of water and my squeegee and run out to the streetlight and wash the Blue Jet—that's what I call the car that the man drives. He reaches out his window and gives me a thumbs-up and a dollar for the day's work. "Thanks," I tell him, and to have a good day. He tells me he will see me again tomorrow. I say, "I hope so." I am happy he is happy and I can have my coffee now. A block away is the caboose, and the people in there are very nice to me. They have good joe. I walk down the street, I see people looking at me. I don't look the best. I look dirty, I guess. This one man says to me, "Why don't you take a bath?" Another one says, "Why don't you go somewhere that no one can see you? You are a disgrace to this city." I keep walking and I do say, "It's been a while since I took a bath, but your mouth's dirtier." I usually quit and keep to myself, but that bothers me. I know it's not an easy life, but it's harder when you got people that act like that. I try to get a bath at least once a week. I have to make money to get a place to stay so I can clean up. It all takes time to be able to do that. I will when I get a chance to wash more windows on cars today and hope to make enough to get a place to clean up. I used to go to the fire station to use one of their firehoses, but they stopped me from doing that because I wasn't a fireman so the boss said I had to leave. I left and haven't since gotten a bath. It's been a month or so since I have taken a bath. Maybe I could use a hose from one of the gas stations to clean up. Well, I will try that, see what happens. Most stations have outdoor bathrooms to use, but you have to ask for the key to get into it. I hope maybe today I can get a yes on that. I hope so. I will just go down another block to the fill station and ask for the key.

I am on my way over there, and I wait for a car to go by and then I am crossing the street. I see a few people but they don't say anything to me, so that is good anyway. I go up to the door and it is open, so I go in and ask for a key. The man in there is busy with someone, so I wait outside until he is done with him. The customer is done and leaves. I go in again to ask and the phone rings. So I go back outside to let him talk on phone without me in there. I notice he is done on the phone, so I try it again, go in, and he says to wait a minute for him. I think it is funny 'cuz I waited for a month to get cleaned up. I am patient and I am waiting for him. He goes into the shop for something, and then he comes back in with a key and hands it to me and says, "Go clean up. Here is some soup and a towel. When you're done in there, please clean up your mess in the bathroom. Thanks, I will talk to you after you do that." I like it, it's like he knew what I was looking to do so he helped me out today.

So I go into bathroom and clean my face and hands with warm soap and water. I do lock the door behind me, so I do take off my pants and shirt and clean myself up. I do have an old comb in my pocket, so I clean up my hair and give it a comb. I do put my polo hat back on and shirt and pants back on. I then clean up the sink, get the dirt out of it, and go out the door. I feel like a new man after that. I go back into the gas station and the man says, "Now I can visit with you. Thanks for doing that. So what can I do for you?" I say, "That's what I came to do today. When I came to your station, it was to clean up." He says, "Well, you can come here any time you need to clean up. I own the place and you seem to be an okay guy that just needed to clean up after a month, hey." I laugh a little bit. He says he has seen me before and was happy to see me come to his place to clean up. He asks if I want to have a cup of coffee with him. I say, "I would, that would be great." So he says to have a seat and let's talk. He starts to talk to me and I just listen to what he has to say.

"First of all, I want to introduce myself." He says his name is Darrel and he owns this shop of his own, works on cars with gas and oil gauges, and changes spark plugs and small stuff like that. "If there's anything else someone needs, I will get it done for them. I work hard to support my family, I always have. I took care of my family when I was fifteen years old. I took care of my brothers and my grandparents. My own parents were on drugs and alcohol and eventually got busted and sent to prison for twenty years. I think they are out now, but I haven't looked them up. I'm still upset with them but life, it is too short, so maybe I will soon. Well, I have told you a little about me, so how about you, what's your life about?"

I am shocked. I think it's my oldest brother, and does he know who I am? Do I dare tell him who I am or what? "I don't know where to start," I tell him. He says, "Well, start with your name." "Well, I'm Tom and I've been away for a while and I have been looking for my family. I live day by day, do what I need to do to survive. I live up by the woods. I have a place up on the hillside. I live alone and I like campfires. I work what I can to have food for myself. I wash car windows. I like it, but maybe I can find more windows to wash today to find a bike to buy. It would help me get around better than when I walk all the time." So I take another sip of coffee and wait to hear what more he has to say. Then the phone rings and he says, "Stay there. I will answer the phone and get back to you, hang on."

While I sit and wait to talk to him again, I start thinking about my childhood again and think of my oldest brother. Darrel, he was a straight-up guy. He worked hard to help us out. I didn't really see it when I was a kid. I can see it now, watching him handle a phone while customers come through the door, bringing in their cars. I thought he was an asshole as a kid, but he seems to be a busy guy. If he doesn't know who I am, maybe I should leave it as that. I don't want to bother him. I don't know what he would think of me now. I look like I am a homeless guy, but in my mind I do have a place. It's a lean-to, but it does keep me dry and I don't want a dime from him. I would think I owed him for my life or something. I would be bothering him if I tell him who am I. I want to really find out if he's my brother, but I don't want him to know it's me. I haven't seen him since I was about nine, close to ten years old. I stayed away from my family for a long time. I have my reasons. I'd rather have him see me as a guy that needs a bath. I don't want to give my life to him, at least not yet. I really want to find out if he is my brother, though. Well, I will let him talk and I will listen, and then I will find out who he is. The way people talk to him, he is pretty well known around town. I don't want to make a bad rep toward him. I don't need anyone to know me around here. I been in town up on the hillside for six months. I didn't know it was my brother's station. My mind is full of thoughts. I need to get back to my fire tonight and talk about it. I'm nervous about finding out, but I know I got to. I won't tell him who I am, though. Just listen today.

The customers leave and he is off the phone. Here he comes, what is he going to ask me now? "Well, I'm back. It's busy and I need a beer. I need to have a beer when I'm done. Well, anyway. How's it going? You said your name once to me, was it Tom, you say?"

I say, "Yes, that's my name."

"Yeah, I had a brother named Tom. Yeah, I don't know what has happened to him. I didn't see him in a long time, well, since we were kids. He was a quiet guy. He lived with my aunt and uncle when he was young. Then he left them and went on his own somewhere, and I haven't kept in touch at all. I do think of him now and then. I wish he would figure it all out and get in touch with us. I don't know, I like the kid. He was just quiet, you didn't know where was in his mind a place. He was messed up when we were kids. .

It was tough on us when Mom and Dad got caught with drugs. Our whole family got torn apart. I kept working for neighbors and people we knew to take care of their places and paint and shovel shit out of their yards, shovel snow. I replaced shingles for the neighbor guy down the road. He gave us money for food and kept up with the bills and especially the roof over our head, the rent. The landlord wanted to get rid of us 'cuz of our parents' issues. Well, I kept it together the best I could. Here I go, rambling on about my past. Well, I do have a beer after work and I think of my brothers. Do you have anything to say more to me?"

"I just got one thing to say to you."

"What's that, Tom?"

"Well, you remind me of my brother, how he took care of us when we were young. He was a good man. Your name is Darrel?"

"Yeah, that's my name, Darrel Buddy. Hey, more people are coming in. If you need the bathroom again, just stop by and get the key, k?"

"All right, thanks, Darrel, will do."

I have to get out of here. I am getting the fuzzy feeling again, like he will figure it out soon. I leave out of there and head down the street, shaking my head. Oh, boy, it was my brother and I don't know what to tell him. Maybe another day. It takes time to tell a lifetime, but not today.

Well, I don't go to the caboose today, instead I met my brother. I keep my buck and head back up the hillside to my place. I need to think about it all. I need to go. I will think about my others later.

I am back up the hill at my site. I have a lot to take in today. I need a nap on my bench. I lie down and take a nap. I can nap when

I need to think. I close my eyes and think about my day. In the mean-time, while I am napping on the bench, this squirrel is up in the tree above me, racing up and down the tree. It is relaxing but annoying at the same time. I am tryin' to nap, but he is bothering me. I yell out to him to shut up, let me sleep. He stops for a moment. Then he starts to race up and down the tree again. I am having a blowing moment in my mind. I am thinking too much about my life. It is getting to me. I like my squirrels, but they can piss me off. I take it as it comes. I need a moment of silence. Please, let me have that moment.

The squirrel stops and chatters at me on the limb above me. My mind is in overdrive and needs to settle down and count backward from a thousand. *One thousand, 999, 998, 987, 996,* okay, I'm start-ing to calm down. I start to get tired. My mind is starting to relax. *995, 994, 993, 992, 991, 990, okay, squirrel, I'm sorry to yell at you. I will relax and take a nap. I get high anxiety a lot, Pete the squirrel. Sorry, Pete.*

When I wake up from my nap, I feel better. I had calmed down. I then start to think about my brother Darrel and how he did in life. He did good. I am happy for him. He was always a hard worker. He was always good to people.

Narrator moment: It's been a good story so far, hasn't it? I hope you are reading to enjoy it. I will be back with the story in a bit. Well, I'm back. I had to have a cup of coffee. I want to keep typing up the story so you don't get bored with it. Well, I want to type about his other brother. I hope you will enjoy reading it.

Yes, I wake up and I am thinking about my other brother Randel. Well, I don't think he is around these parts of the country, but maybe he is. I will try to look him up in the newspapers to see if he is in the ring. It's a big city to find out. I believe they have boxing here. I will gather up some wood for tonight and head for town again.

I get enough wood for tonight. I am on my way to the city from the hillside. I hope to find a bit about him. If not I will move on tomorrow.

I get down to the highway and cross it. I get down the overpass and head down town, go through a couple of stoplights, turn, and head down a street that has a bus route. I find a bench and a garbage can and look through it to find a newspaper. I look and don't find any, so I go to another one a block away and find one. I have at least half of it but no sports paper. Well, I will look again. There is another basket and I find another newspaper. It is the sports page. I look in it. I see football and baseball results. I look some more and I find a page on boxing. I look at a few pictures and a few names, but I can't find anyone with the name Red in it. I look to see if I can find Randel, but I don't see any name. Well, I can always look tomorrow morning. So I go back up the hillside and sit on my bench. I am tired and sad about it. Well, maybe another paper will have him in it. I hope so.

Well, it is getting dark and I am getting the chills. I start a fire. I am still thinking about him. I wonder if he is in any magazines. Maybe he is. It's hard to get a mag, but maybe I do have enough money to get one. It's got to be a dollar. Well, in the morning I can get enough bucks washing the Blue Jet and have enough money for one. Hoping to find what I'm looking for, I add a few more pieces of wood to the fire and head to bed. I think of him boxing big time.

Morning comes and I slept good. I am now heading down the hillside to go to town again. I get down to the stoplight, where I see the Blue Jet, and wash his windows. I receive another buck. I tell him thank you, and he puts up the thumb and says thanks. I then head down the street a couple of blocks, and at the end of the block is the magazine store. I go in and I look around the shelves and find a magazine of sports. I look through quickly, can't find any boxing, look for another one, and the desk clerk asks if I need any help. I tell him that I am looking for a boxing magazine. He tells me that it is on the bottom shelf to the left, and I look. I see it and look in it for a second. I look for his name, and the clerk asks me if I am done looking. I think he wants me out of his store. I think he thinks I don't have any money to buy one. I do have the money, and I go to the counter and give what I have. I give him two bucks for it and he gives me fifty cents back. I think that is a good deal and I still can go to the caboose and have my morning coffee. So I tell him thank you and head out of the store.

I go back toward the stoplight and cross the street to the caboose. I then see people looking at me like I stole the magazine. I feel like I am an inch tall. I feel so good that I worked for the money and was able to get it. What the hell do they know, anyway? I can't worry about that right now. I have to look for my brother's name.

So I get to the caboose and walk in. The waitress says hi and to sit where I want to in here. So I sit next to the window, and she comes by and asks want I want. I tell her, "Coffee and cream and sugar, please."

"Coming right up," she says. I say thanks. I take out the mag and look in it. I stare at the beginning page and look through it, and I get to the middle of the page and what do I see? My brother Randel, the Red Fist himself. He looks tough. I think that is good, and he is a prize fighter. A real fighter. He looks great and he won his last match. He looks proud in the picture. I wish I was there. Where is there in the state of Missouri, Kansas City, MS? What a picture, hey, I tell the waitress as she approaches me with my coffee. She says, "Oh, Red FIST, yeah, I know him."

"You do? How?"

"My sister dated him for a bit."

"Oh, what happened?"

"She wanted to settle down and he wasn't going to. He wanted to fight in the big-time prize fight. He was a good guy, I liked him. Randel was a good man."

"Well, that's cool. You don't know where he is now, do you?"

"Well, the last I heard he was in Colorado. But I think his next fight was out in New York, I believe."

"Cool, thanks," I say.

I sip my coffee and look through the magazine some more and see a few more clips of him. What I would do if I saw his next fight.

I need to get to New York, and I will leave tomorrow or the next day. I like to travel at night. I travel by train. I like trains. I'm in Seattle and I need to get to New York. Well, I need to plan now for it. Don't need much. I sip down the rest of my coffee and leave the rest of the money for a tip. Head out the door and tell her thanks for the info.

I go back to the hillside for the rest of the day. I sit on the bench up there and think of my brother, Red. So cool, my brother, a big-time prize fighter. I love it. It's so great to know he is doing good. Well, don't need much to pack for the trip. I will just get some food in the garbage behind the caboose in the morning. I am hungry now. Well, it's sometime in the late afternoon. I need to get there to eat the supper meals. So I head back down into the city and go back to the caboose in the back of it. I find the garbage can and look. I find a half-eaten burger and some fries. I eat them right there. It is good and filling.

I find some apples in there, too. They have a couple of bites out of them. So I grab one and put it into my pocket for later tonight. I find a pop can that has a few sips out of it, so I drink that, it is good. I have my food for the night and got an apple in my pocket for later. I should be good till tomorrow afternoon or so. Well, I head back up the hillside for now and wait till dark to catch the train. I have my fire ready for a bit and sit on my bench. I take a nap. I am ready to go for a ride on the rails. It's been a while since I've been on one, at least six months, so it's getting chilly out and the fire is low. I better get going if I'm going to catch the midnight express. Common name for a night train.

I go down the hillside and into town, past the lights, and at the end of the back end of town, about twelve blocks. The lights are getting lower as you get farther away from downtown. On your left is the airport. On your right there is the railyard. I cross over the road and go to a fence. I see an open area of the fence and crawl through it. I'm in the railyard now. Dark around here. That's good, it needs to be for me so no one sees me cross the way. I start to cross over the tracks and a few more, another set of tracks. I then come upon a string of boxcars on a track. They aren't the ones that I am going to get on. I go through a few more tracks of cars and get to the mainline, a few lights but I am still in the shadows. I hear a train whistle in the distance. I don't know if that's the midnight train or not. I can tell by the size of locomotive they are. The big ones are road-powered and the small ones are for switching or short trips in the city, transfer jobs. They go around to the industries and elevators for the grain. You can hear the whistles at night from the hillside. It's nice when you're at the fire and the moon is bright, and you look at the stars and listen for the mighty night train. It's really cool. I used to have a harmonica to play, but I gave it to a guy for the jacket I'm wearing. I was cold and needed it. I might find another one someday. I might trade my coat for it or a pair of gloves for it. We will see when the time comes.

I'm hearing the whistle getting closer, and it's louder than a switcher. I see the bright light of the engine, and I hope it's the one I'm looking for and it's going by me now. Wow, what a sound up closer than the hillside. I see it. I see that the train is bigger. It is oil cars and grain cars and auto cars. I do see a few boxcar doors are closed on it, though. Well, I will keep looking. I see more cars in the light, and there are a few boxcars and the doors are open and I will get on one of them, and I started to run across to the r-train and I hear the train coming to a stop. The sound of smashing cars is pretty cool. I get   to the boxcars and get in front of the one I want to ride on. I crawl into it and I get into the back of it so nobody sees me in there. I need this train trip and lay low until I'm out of town. I feel the train move again. I hear the cars stretch out, and here we go. It's starting out slowly and picks up speed quickly. I am riding the rails to go see my brother's fight. I hope I make it.

I close the door on the backer a little bit. You don't want to close it all the way or you will be stuck in there for a long time. I find out a few died in there 'cuz of that, so I shut it a little bit. I sit on the floor and look out the door. We are going by the depot, and I move back into the dark part of the car. Good, no one has seen me, I hope not. I need this ride. I hope I get to the next station. The next stop should be in Chicago, I believe. I believe I have to wait till trade crews and go again. I'll just relax here, and it's a bit before we get to Chicago.

I am sitting in the boxcar with a few crates. Behind one of the crates there is a dog. The dog looks at me and has a whine to him. He is a yellow lab or something like that. It weighs about fifty pounds or so. I like dogs. I used to have a dog growing up, and it was a yellow lab. His name was Rusty. He was a good dog, very protective. He went everywhere with me while I had him. He was hit by a car when I was young. It was sad but I enjoyed him while I had him in my life. This dog seems to like me. I am wondering how he got here on the train. I wonder how far he traveled. He had to have at least traveled a hundred miles. Well, he must have not have anyone in his life or he probably would have stayed. I like him, so I will call him Boxcar, good household name. I think, anyway. I hope he wants to hang out with me for a bit anyway, that would be very cool. Well, I have that apple in my pocket, so I will feed him, that is if he wants it. "Well, here you go, little fella, try some apple." I open my hand and put it out there for him, and he takes a smell and he grabs it and eats part of it. He is very happy. He waves his tail. I figured he would 'cuz he went so far without food. I feel bad for him. I hope he sticks with me. We would be a good team, him and I. I called out, "Boxcar," and he looks sharply at me. I think he liked the name I gave him. He waves his tail, and I think it is very cool. He decides to sit next to me, and we both look out the door and see a few trees and some rolling hills. I notice a big bridge is coming up. We are going to go over a bridge and over a river, and we see big hills along the river. What a view, what an awesome view. I like it and I get a friend to enjoy it with me. I hope we stop soon. I need some food to eat, both of us together. We are a team now. It keeps my spirits up. I think we will be together for a while.

Anyway, I hope it will be great. I like having a friend to hang with throughout the day. I think he likes my companionship, too. I enjoy Boxcar, and it's getting dark now. We are still moving across the country on the rails. Well, maybe we can nap a bit. "Well, Boxcar, let's nap. I need a nap now." I'm lying down with my friend. Thinking about my life. Thinking of my past and now future. "I'm tired, Boxcar, I can tell you are, too. See ya when we wake."

I need a narrator moment, please. I'm thinking about the story now. We have a homeless guy on the train with a dog that ate a part of an apple that he had in his pocket and it was for later, when he got it out of a garbage can in Seattle. Some throw a good apple away, and it just saved the dog's life. If you think about it, pretty cool, hey. I think so. Well, I think we should get to the story of Tom and Boxcar Buddy's fun, hey, I think so. Where will the adventure go now with them both? Let's see now. Where were we? What will them face together now?

"Well, Boxcar, I think we are waking up to another city here. Let's see what the sign says as we go by it. It says 'Whitefish.' Wow, Whitefish, Montana, very pretty, look at the mountains. Look, Boxcar, look. What a view." Well, the train is slowing down a bit. I wonder if it's going to stop here for a bit. It's stopping all right. I feel the train bunching up and I hear the brakes on the wheels squeaking. "We better hang on, Boxcar." Yes, it's stopped now. I bet we have a few minutes before it starts up again. They must be switching crews or something. "Okay, Boxcar, let's get out for a bit, see if we can find some food for the rest of the trip or at least till we stop again."

We get out of the boxcar and head into the woods. We are in the woods and we need to find berries or something. We walk a bit and we do find some berries. We pick some, they look like huckleberries. That's cool, and they are very good. But we have to be careful 'cuz where berries are so are the bears. Big bears, grizzles and mountain lions. "Let's hurry, pick what we can put into our pockets and get the hell out of here." We pick, eat a few, get my pockets filled, and now let's go. We start back to the train for our boxcar and we get back in. We shut the door a little bit. Now I hear the brakes released, and now it's stretching out the cars and we start to move. We are now picking up speed again, and we are on our way again. Let's hope we make it to the next stop. We need some water soon. Well, our next stop is in North Dakota, I believe. Fargo or Grand Forks, don't know off hand which way. We are seeing some mountains and it's so pretty out here. Going over another bridge, and it looks like a tunnel coming up. Wow, right through the mountains. Cool, very cool. "Well, it's going to be dark in there for a bit, Boxcar. I hope you don't mind the dark." I laugh when I say that. Well, it's dark and cool. I feel the turn of wheels, or I should say the bending of them. Must be going (illegible) and it straightens out and I see the end of the tunnel, some light. It's bright and we are now out of the tunnel. Wow, all I see is mountains, trees up above us. The train is really slowing down now. Must be going up the mountain again, or I should say still going up since we left. I like it. "Boxcar, do you like it, too? I think you do," and he yelps and barks. Now it's starting to get dark again, we need to nap a bit. We hear the clickity-clack of the wheels and we see the moon, bright out tonight. We see the stars out there, pretty cool. Up and down the mountain we've been going. I like it. I'm nodding off a bit, and I'm out for the count. So is Boxcar.

Morning comes and here the train slows down again, and it's bunching up. I think we are stopping again. "Yep, Boxcar, we are." It comes to a stop and I say to Boxcar, "Look, there is a lake out in front of us. Let's get out for a bit. I need some water, don't you, Boxcar?" We get out of the car and head to the lake. It is a clear lake and there is a stream flowing into it. "Let's go over there." We go off to the stream and I cup my hands and get some water and drink some. It is good, and Boxcar goes into the water and swims around a bit. It is cool to see him do that. It reminds me of my Rusty growing up. He liked the water, too. We did live by a lake, and I would go over to it and fish in it as a kid. Spent a lot of time doing that as a kid. It was lots of fun. So it just brings back memories for me. I do get emotional about it. My dog did get hit by a car. A day when I was over to the lake and we were on the way back to the house, and it happened by the house. I was very sad about it. I am glad there isn't a road by here, anyway. "Well, we better get back to the train, Boxcar, before it leaves without us. Let's hurry, Boxcar."

Well, we make it to the train and we get back on it. I am glad I have Boxcar with me. I really enjoy his company. I think he enjoys mine, too. We can feel the train stretch out, and off we go again. It's picking up speed, and I am happy we are. We need to stop again to get some more food. I notice the mountains are gone but a lot of fields, we must be in the state of North Dakota. I think we are going or coming up to Fargo, ND. It's a quiet area. Lots of farmers. Tractors and some corn, it looks like. I like corn. Maybe we will stop soon again next to a field of corn so we can get some. Wait a second, the train is slowing down a bit and we are coming to a stop. Maybe they got some work to do here. I see an elevator. They are dropping off a few cars, I think. Yes, they are stopped and they are setting some cars out to the elevator. "We will be here for a bit. So let's get out."

Boxcar and I get out of the boxcar and head toward the corn in the field. It looks like sweet corn, so let's get a few ears. We grab about twenty of them and get back on the train. We have enough to eat for three days, I think. Well, I can eat some right now. "You hungry, Boxcar?" I believe he is. "Well, let's have some corn." It's good, fresh. I take the stalk off and take a bite of it. It is great and it will be filling. I take a little pocket knife out of my pocket. I peel the corn of the husk. I give some to Boxcar. He eats some. He is hungry. So we eat a lot of corn while waiting for the train to go again. It is a nice day out, little breeze and a few clouds. Sun is out, that is good.

The train gets back together and I can hear the air go through the cars. The train is shorter now. We hope it will not get too much shorter, or they will see us back here. Well, I guess we are on our way. The train is stretched out and moving again. It's picking up speed, and we are on a roll. Clickity-clonk. Clickity-clank. The wheels are turning; it's a nice, relaxing sound. Our bellies are full now, and it's naptime for a bit. I think the next stop will be in Minnesota—Minneapolis, MN. It's a big railyard. I hope the train keeps going tonight. Boxcar is lying down and he is going to take a nap, too.

Narrator moment: I'm having a cup of coffee and thinking about what I'm telling here. It's good, isn't it? I hope you are on your edge of your seat. You can't shut the light off, you can't put the book down. I wouldn't yet; there is more to read. I hope you're enjoying it. Here we go again. You got the two of them napping after eating some North Dakota corn, that's sweet corn, people. While on the high iron, they are in a boxcar with the door partly closed. The sun is starting to go down.

I wake up from a nap and Boxcar is already up, looking out of the boxcar. He is looking at a nice view with the sunset. I like it. I think it is great. I think we will have to take a picture someday when I get a camera. I just remember it in my mind. I think Boxcar does the same. The sun is getting farther down below the few trees we see. Before you know it, it will be dark again and we will see a few stars out again. It's a warm night out, anyway. I think it's cool.

It does get dark out. The moon is shining on the rails. You can see the stars. Boxcar seems to be hungry, so I give him more corn. He eats a little bit, and I eat the rest of the ear. It is good. We now have about eight ears left of corn. We have enough for the morning and maybe for lunch, anyway. I hope to find some water on the next stop. I'm getting thirsty and I think Boxcar is, too. I hope we take a longer break this time. I have to figure out if this train keeps going through or not. I hope it does, but if not we can find another one to ride on in

Minneapolis. It will be okay. Lots of trains coming up, maybe we can get on one toward Iowa and have more sweet corn in a few days. We need to get to Chicago. That's where we need to be. I think if we go to another yard, it will bring us there. I have to see in a bit. We do stop a lot through other cities coming up, maybe we can get on another train on a different track. There is another small town in Minnesota, it's called Detroit Lakes. The other railroad meets up there with them. They cross over the tracks that we are on now. We will see if they stop or at least slow down to get off. It's been a while since I was in that area by train. It will be morning by the time we get there. They will come up and I think it might stop there. Let's hope so.

The sun is about to come up now, and I see we are coming up to the area. I can see a signal and it's yellow. "I think we are in luck, Boxcar." I hope to get off this one. We are only a couple of miles out from that next signal. Yes, the train is slowing up. It seems to come to a stop in a mile or so. Yes, it's slowing up a lot. I see in the distance that the light of that signal is red. "It's going to stop, Boxcar, are you ready to get off in a second? Let's throw the corn out. Let's not forget that that's our food." I throw that corn out of the boxcar, and I jump out and so does Boxcar. It takes a bit for Boxcar. At first I think he isn't going to. He does. He must really like me. I guess; I feed him. We are now in Detroit Lakes, MN. The train again is on the move, and we are waiting for it.

I got to get by us, then we can walk the tracks into town anyway. It's by us and we are walking. I hope to see the other train ahead of us to go another way. We have come up to the other signal and no train yet. We can wait here for it.

We decide to sit and wait for another train to go south. While we wait we decide to eat more corn. We are eating sweet corn from North Dakota. We are sitting under an overpass. We see a lot of cars and trucks. We've been seeing other trains that go by and head west. Those are not the ones we need. It might be a bit. There is a building just down the tracks. Maybe we can get some water from there. "Let's go see, Boxcar." We head down the tracks and it's an old depot. I don't see any cars there, maybe we are in luck. Let's get closer. I see and hear some people talking over by the depot. Maybe they do work there. I can go ask if they got any water for us. Doesn't hurt to ask. Let's see how they act.

We go up to a man that is wearing bibs. He has an old hat on. It looks greasy. He is the man to ask, I think.

"Well, hi, guy, is there any way we could get some water? We are thirsty."

"For you guys, I can do that for you. Come with me."

We go up to the door of the depot. We decide to wait outside. The man goes in and he comes out with bottles of water, four for us.

"Thanks, man, for the water." I'm glad he is nice to us.

He says, "No problem, guy."

"We are just waiting for a train to go by so we can get back to work on the tracks. Thanks again," I say.

We head back under the overpass. He does yell out to us that the train should be here in about thirty minutes or so. "Okay," I tell him, "thanks." Good info. "We'll just wait here for it, Boxcar." I figure we should hear it soon. We have some water and put the rest in our pockets, my pockets, I laugh out loud. I dig a little hole in the ground and pour a bit of water in it for Boxcar and he drinks it up. I give him some more and he is wagging his tail. He is happy. I think I hear a whistle in the distance. I do hear it and it is getting closer. I have a little corn with some water to drink, ready to get on the train. I hear it coming around the bend. It's slowing down. I see the light boxcar. "Let's get ready to hop on the train." I now see the light. It's almost stopped. It's still moving toward us. We hide and crouch down under the overpass.

That train is starting to move a little faster. It's almost by us. "Get that engine by us, and then we will stand here and wait for the right car to jump on." The train is by us, and it is going slow enough to jump on. We walk toward the train, alongside it, and they are almost all tank cars. All I see are tanks. I now see lumber cars. I now see refrigerator cars. There are a few boxcars but no doors open. Now all I see is autocars, can't get into those. Okay, okay, now I see something. It's a boxcar, and the door is open. It's an empty car. Well, some stuff is in it. But we can still get into it. "Let's go, Boxcar, let's get into that one." I climb up on the ladder and Boxcar just sits there. "Come on, Boxcar, get in. Let's go, buddy. Get in, let's go." He sits there and doesn't want to go in the car. Well, I bail out of the car. I probably should have gone, but I can't leave Boxcar. Damn dog. Well, let's look, maybe we still have another chance. I don't see any more cars to get into. There is the end of the train. "Dammit, Boxcar, we could have taken it. What's wrong with you?" Boxcar lies down, puts his head on his paw, and looks like he isn't wanting to go. I understand; the train was moving. He wasn't going to jump into it while it moved, I guess. Well, I hope another one comes by soon. Probably not for the rest of the day, though. I hope it will be tonight. We start to walk into town, following east. I believe we have to get the one train that goes where we were going before. We will hear one soon. We saw a few a bit ago, hope to get one going east.

"I hear one coming, Boxcar, are you ready this time?" The signal is all red. But that's for trains going west. We need them to stop and be heading east. "Let's go ahead toward the other side of the lights."

We head west on the tracks and get on the other side of lights. I see red lights on this side. Maybe we will get lucky this time and they will stop here. I'm hoping, anyway. "Well, let's get ready, Boxcar, and I hope you come with me on this next one. I'm going with or without you. I need to keep moving toward New York, k? Well, I hear one and I see the light of the train. It's getting closer. Let's get ready this time. I need to get going on this one, Boxcar. Okay, it's here and let's do it."

The train comes to a stop, and we head to toward the tail end of the train, looking for an open boxcar to climb in. Don't see any yet.

I'm still looking for one. "Keep walking, Boxcar. Wait a minute, I see a boxcar and the door is open. Let's go for it, Boxcar, come on." I climb in and Boxcar does jump into it this time. "Good boy, thanks for coming, boy. I would have missed you." We get into to it and it starts to move and we take a seat. It's picking up speed. I close the door on it a bit. We are looking out the door and we see the town. It is a small town but has a lot of lights and oh, boy, a big lake. "That's pretty cool, hey, Boxcar." Boxcar goes into the corner of the car and I don't know why he does that, but he feels bad about something. "Well, are you happy to be with me, boy?" He wags his tail. He'll be okay. I hope, anyway. Maybe he is from here, that small town. Maybe he really is home. I guess I didn't think of that. "Well, it will be okay, boy. If the train stops, maybe we can get off. And we can go back to the town." The train is going ahead and is picking up speed. We won't be anywhere near that town, we better just stay on here. "Well, let's take a nap and not worry about it. We got each other, bud. I love you, Boxcar, and I will take care of you. Stick with me, Boxcar." Boxcar wags his tail. It's started to get dark out, and the sun is down. We are on our way toward Minneapolis, MN. I hope we get there soon, and I hope this train keeps going toward Chicago. "Let's nap a bit, Boxcar."

It's dark out, and I'm hungry and thirsty, and I take out some last of the corn and eat it and I do give some to Boxcar, but he doesn't want any. He turns down food, he is not feeling good. I cut open the water bottle at the top and drink it and cut a little more so Boxcar can get his mouth in it and have a drink. He comes over and takes a drink and goes back to the corner of the car. "Okay I see how you are, bud. I will just leave it for you for later, and I hope you drink some more when you want to." I just kick back and tilt my hat forward and over my eyes for some shuteye.

The sun comes up and we are coming into another city, but it isn't Minneapolis. I don't know what city it is, give me a moment. Oh, it's St. Cloud. The train is still moving along. It's not stopping for the city.

I wonder where they are going. Well, I will find out soon. The train is slowing down but isn't stopping. I see another train alongside it. It's going by us fast. I guess we are still moving on to the next town. I notice that the train is slowing down so more. Oh, this is a siding that they are in. I understand now. They are coming to a stop in a bit. The train is stopping, and I see another headlight of another train. We are stopped and waiting for that train to pass. The train is now going by us, and I see the end of the train. I think we will be moving again soon. Now it's been a bit and we are not moving. Oh, I see another train coming toward us. It's going by us fast. That's a short train. I hear the air on the train. It's releasing the brakes and it's starting to move. We are moving on again. We are picking up speed and we are now heading toward Minneapolis. I hope we make it there. I need a break from these trains for a bit. "Let's check out the city when we get there, Boxcar. I hope you like it when we see the big city. Maybe we can spend the night in the city, get some food and more water. I will find a hillside and make a fire with you, Boxcar. Would you like that, hang out with me at a warm fire? Well, I will show you the city. It's been a while since I've been there, so things have probably changed a lot. It will be great. I will wash a few windows, get some money, and have a meal by the fire. It's been a long trip on the rails. We do need a break; you don't feel good and I think you need some good food. Let's hope it's going to be good. As long as I have you to hang with, it will be great."

The sun is bright and we see the shining of the rail ahead, and we see the light of the tracks. Lots of signals ahead, we must be getting into the yard soon. "Well, let's get ready to get off this train, Boxcar." The train is slowing up. We are entering the yard. It's a big yard, I see twenty tracks or so. We need to bail out soon. It's coming to a stop, and we are ready to jump off. It's stopped and we jump out of the boxcar and onto the tracks. We start heading across the tracks. We are heading toward the big buildings. I see an overpass to the left of us and a bridge to the right of us. I think it's the Mississippi River or St. Croix. "Well, let's go this way, toward the river. I can get under the bridge. Okay, Boxcar, let's go and get under the bridge." We are close to the bridge and we see another train that is going by us, and we have to wait for it to go by us. It does and it is a small train engine and a few cars. "There is the bridge, and let's get under it." We go under the bridge, and there is the riverbed. I notice there are a few people that are here. I see an old fire spot. It was a small fire that was put out. I look for a few pieces of wood. I see and use some old pieces of wood that are burnt a little. I take out my knife and peel a piece of wood. I make some kindling. It will start easy, it is dry wood. Now I need some paper or bark. I do see some paper plates and cups and some leaves from the trees above that have blown off the tress above us. I gather up the stuff and bring it over to the firewood. I put it under the kindling and start the fire with a match that I had in my pocket. I have a few in there from before. I don't use much. I hope I keep it started with one match. Well, I start it going. I blow on it a bit and we have flames. It's going and a little more wood and more and it's bigger. I add the burnt piece of wood and it is dry and it's light. "We are okay, Boxcar." We get flames and it's nice but we need more wood. "Let's find some more along the river." I see some wood and I get it. It's dry, it will burn. I get some more and my arms are full and go back to the fire and put a little on it, and then I sit down on the ground. Boxcar sits next to me for a moment, then he sits behind me. He is tired. I will let him nap and I think I will do the same. I lie back, put my hat over my eyes, and I fall asleep. Fire is warm. I need more wood in a bit.

Narrator moment: You liking the story that I'm telling? I hope so. I need some coffee to keep going with the story. Let's see, Tom and Boxcar make it to Minneapolis, Minnesota. They are now under a bridge along the Mississippi. They took a nap, now they are awake and here we go.

"Hey, Boxcar, what are you doing over there? Come back here. I need to get you some food. I need you. Come here, boy." Boxcar is about a half a mile up the river. I can see him in the distance. I hope he isn't leaving me, but for some reason he isn't coming back. Well, I will go get him. I get up and head toward him. Boxcar stops and sees me heading toward him. He wags his tail.

I look at him and start walking toward him. He goes up the hill. I follow him up the bank, and on the top there is a road and Boxcar crosses it, and I am following him across the road. We are getting into the city. There is traffic. I am nervous he is going to get hit by a car. I see him running down the road. He is next to a building. There are a couple of people walking around the building. He follows them. I finally get across the road and down to the building where Boxcar is. I get around the building and a couple of guys are throwing sticks and rocks at Boxcar. I yell out at them to stop doing that, and they look at me and say, "What are you going to do about it?" I'm not a violent man. I am not going to fight them, but I say they are a couple of big guys and they should leave a dog alone. It's my dog. They laugh and they come after me and I stand my ground. They come swinging at me, and I go after them. I take out my knife and tell them to leave, and they take out another knife they have. They swing it at me and they stuck me with a knife in my arm. Boxcar comes at them and jumps on them. He goes after their necks, and the one stabs him in the chest. Boxcar yelps and falls to the ground, and I get up and kick at them and pull them off of Boxcar. I stab the one in the leg, and he falls to the ground. The man leaves and runs around the building. I kick the guy in the head. I'm not a violent man, but I don't like those guys picking on my dog. A guy gets up and hops away toward the other side of the building and disappears. I go to Boxcar and he is breathing. I am worried about him. He doesn't move much. I pick him up and carry him. I carry him over to the riverbank. We go under the bridge, where we were. We are by the fire again. I leave there and go to get more wood. I gather more wood and get the fire going again. I put Boxcar by the fire. He doesn't move. He is not breathing. He is dead. I check to see if he has a pulse and he doesn't. I lose another dog in my life. We should have stayed on the train. We should have gone on to another town. I feel bad now. I now don't want to go anywhere anymore. I will just stay here and just beg for food. I don't care. My mind is racing, I am upset with myself. I don't handle death too good. We should have moved on by train. I should have left in another town. I should let him go home. I'm hurting and I was wrong. I shouldn't blame myself for it. I don't know what to do and more. I need to go to bed for a bit. I need to bury him. I carry him down the riverbank. I dig a hole with my hands and put him in it. I then bury him. I pray a bit for him. I tell him I am sorry and I am very sad. I then go back to the fire. I lie back and put my hat down over my eyes and sleep. I am out cold.

I awake and get up off the ground and go for a walk around the bridge. I sit on the riverbank. I am still sad about Boxcar, a friend, a true friend. I liked him. He made me happy. I guess all I can do is thank the good God for letting him into my life for a bit. I miss him lots. I hand him a lot of corn and water. I was on the train with him. He was my bud. Well, I guess I have to move on and never forget him. He did try to save me from those guys. He was a hero. Heroes do die sometimes. He was a good dog. I must remember the good times I had with him and move on. It's okay, he was my friend and I lost him. I clean up my wound on my leg. I cut off part of my shirt and tie it around my leg. I will be okay. It will heal. My heart will heal, too. I decide to walk the riverbank. I walk along a bank a bit. I find an old fishing rod. It has a line and reel on it, and I am lucky, I guess. I can cast a line into the river and catch a fish. I need to eat and move on in life. It will be okay.

I am depressed about Boxcar, but I need to push on in life. I dig and find some worms for fishing. I go back to the bridge. Fish like the shade. I now got to find some hooks there, got to be some old line around here. I look and find some. I find a hook on a line. I bite the line and get the hook. I put the line through my rod eyes and have a decent line, and I put the hook on the line. I find a sinker and that line, too. I put it on the line also. I'm ready now. I put the worm on the hook. I then cast the line out. I am fishing. I am fishing on the Mississippi. I hope to catch a fish. It would be a good meal. I sit with my rod in the water and sit on the riverbank. I jiggle it a bit and let it sit. I am waiting patiently for a fish. I think back when I would fish with my grandfather. He taught me how to fish. I miss him a lot. We lost him 'cuz of cancer. He died and I lost my grandfather. I have good memories of him. We fished a lot. We talked a lot. I loved him.

It's now my life and I got to survive. I need a bite now. I sit with my line in the water a bit. I start to think about him again, and the line goes tight. It jiggles and it is a fish, I can feel it. It is a fish now, I must set the hook. I set now and I feel the fish on it. I start to reel it in. It is a fight. I need that fish. I get the fish up to the top of the water. It jumps in the air and it is a cool sight. I keep reeling it in and there is a fish, it is a catfish. Wow, what a fish. It has to be at least five pounds or so. It will be a good meal. Perfect size to eat. I bring the fish up to the fire. I take it off the j-hook. I take out my knife and stab it in the throat. I get it. I then cut out the gills, and I slice the belly open and take out the guts. I then go down to the water and wash it a bit. It is ready to put on a stick. I've done this before. I find a stick and feel it and bend it so it will be strong enough to hold it and not break. It will work. I then find a couple other sticks that are bigger. I break them and have y-looking sticks, and I put them in the ground where I have the fire, one on each side. I put the one I put through the fish on the branches that are over the fire, and I set them up to hold the fish on the branch and spin it. I let it cook on one side and then I turn it to cook the other side. I cook it a bit. It is smoking from the inside out. It's almost done. The grease from the belly of the fish is dripping. It's done and I take it off and go to eat it. I think of Grandpa and take a bite. It is good, and I need to get some more later. I get full. I am happy I have food. I thank God and take a nap. Thinking about my dog and my grandfather, I sleep. I am tired. I sleep till the morning sun comes up. I am still full from the fish. I now can think of what I am going to do for the day.

First I got to write something on the bridge about Boxcar. I find some creosote. I find some off the tracks, above the bridge. I write on the bridge that Boxcar was here. "Rest in peace, Boxcar." It is nice to say that about my friend. I then am thinking about going to wash car windows again. I need to find a busy street.

I head toward town. I find a street that has many lights and one-way ones. I then head toward a garbage can behind a building. I am looking for an old spray bottle. I don't find any in the first garbage can but look in a couple more and find one. I grab it and now I need to find some water to put into the bottle. I look around the buildings. I don't find any, so I walk toward another building and it is a gas station. I find a hose. I figure it will be okay to get some water into the bottle from it. So I fill up the bottle. I spray, it works. So I head back to the busy lights. I also find some paper towels in a small garbage can at the corner of the lights. That will work for now. I need to find the right car to wash the windows. I see a Volkswagen Bug, and that will work for now. I go out to wash it as soon as the light is red. I start to wash the window, and I get that window done. The man in there rolls his window down and says thanks. He doesn't give me any money for doing that, just a wave. I go back to the curb and wait for the right car again. The light turns red and I run out with my spray bottle and spray another windshield, and I start washing the window. That man in there says, "Get the hell away from my car, you bum." Wow, tough crown in Minneapolis. I hope I have better luck at another set of lights.

I then go to another light across the street. It turns red. I go to wash and I get yelled at for being in the road from a woman on the sidewalk. What a bitch. Oh, well, I guess. I spend my time in this street. I move down the road to a different set of lights. I need to get away from those assholes. Well, it will get better soon. The lights turn red and I go out to wash, and I see something out in the street. It is a quarter on the ground. I pick it up. I then put it into my pocket. I start to wash that car, and a man says to me, "Will you wash my whole car for five bucks?" I say sure I will. The man pulls over the car. I start to wash the car.

I wash down the sides and the roof. I wash all the windows and the bumpers, I wash the lights. It is a Nova. It is green, about a '72, maybe. It looks good. The man gives me five bucks, says thanks, and he moves on. I wave and I am hoping to see him again in the area. I put the five bucks in my pocket and start to walk down the street. I come upon another gas station, and I find a fill-up garbage can full of pails. I grab a couple and they look good enough to put water in them and also use them to sit on. It is turning out okay. It's a fine day out.

I go toward the back of the building, down an alley. I see a spout and I get some water out of it. I fill the pail up. I need a squeegee, that would work better. I look in the old garbage in the back. I look and look. I find an old one, the handle is broken off a bit but it will work. I need some soap or something. I find an old bottle that has some leftover soap in the bottom of it. I then put the rest in the pail of water, stir it around, and I have soap, it will work better. I fill up my bottle with that and the soap. I head toward the streetlights again. The lights turn red and I grab my squeegee and bottle and head out to a car. I am at a station wagon and a family is in it. I wash the windows and I receive a dollar from the guy. I thank him and the family says bye. I guess they have a heart for people that need the pay. I like it. I feel better today. I was depressed about Boxcar, but I must move on. I go toward the bridge again, go back underneath it, and I sit a bit. I know I need some food now. I lie down and decide to take a nap. I need to wait until suppertime. I will find a restaurant. I will get good food today. I need to rest my eyes a bit. I pull over my hat and take a nap. The sun is starting to go down, and I need to find a restaurant. I'm hungry. I get up and head to town, and I see a restaurant and in the back of it is where the garbage is. I dive in it and find a half-eaten burger and some leftover chicken. I eat it, it is good and filling. I can't understand people, they throw away good food. But I feel good and filled today, so thank you, people. I am a survivor. I will wash more windows. I hope some of the same cars are around tomorrow. I head back to the bridge. I want to go fishing again. It relaxes me. I need that. I dig up some more worms and get my rod and put it into the river. I am fishing.

It doesn't matter what kind of day you're having, it's like a good day of fishing. My grandpa used to tell me that. I like how he put that. I always think of my grandpa when I go fishing. We had good times together. He took me everywhere. I like to go fishing, and I like to go to the store to get treats. I enjoyed my time with him. We went camping together and we had good fires. It was a good times when I was young, when I was able to get away from my brothers from picking on me. It was a safe place to be. My mind would be at ease. Sometime I can talk about my grandpa and me. I need to get a fire going now. I need some more wood. I will get some and have a good fire tonight. The fish isn't biting right now, but maybe later tonight I will get some. It's still a good day when you're having a bad one. It puts a smile to my face. I'm always at peace in my mind when I fish. I'm getting some wood. I find some dry stuff and some branches. I find some old leaves and some bark off a tree that fell into the river. I can pull branches off of that one. So I get some of that and bring it to the fire. I have a book of matches from before, and I put the leaves and small branches on top. I break up more wood. Small pieces. I can light it now. I take the matches out and light the leaves, they light, and the branches are on the flame, it's started. I then put little bigger pieces on and I have a good flame. What a fire. I can try again for some fish.

I put another worm on the hook and cast it into the river. I jiggle it a little and then I let it sit. I dig a hole to put around it. I put a branch into a Y and I put into the ground and set the rod against that. I then go back up to the fire. I watch the mood and it sits for about thirty minutes. I go down to check it, and the line goes out and I set the hook. I then get a fish at the end of the line. I start to reel it in and it's a good fight. I keep reeling and up comes a fish out of water and flops, and I go down closer to the water and reel it in, grab the fish, and bring up, it is another catfish. It has to be around eight pounds or so. I think it is a good catch for the day. I take it off the line and take out my knife. I cut out the gills and the belly, take out the guts. I then find a good branch and I put it through the fish. I put it on the set of branches that are on each side of the fire, and I am able to turn the fish a little bit at a time. I cook and the belly fat is dripping into the flame. I turn it some more and it is ready to eat. I take it away from the flame. I pull back the skin of the cat and enjoy the meat. It is great. I like it. It fills my belly. I am full after eating it.

I look around me and I find an old can. It is good, no holes in it. I put some water in it from the river, and I put it into the fire to heat up the water and then I can drink it. It takes the bugs out of it. I wait for it to boil, then I take it off the fire and let it cool a bit. I then give it a drink out of the can. It is good. I will make it another day. My grandfather used to say it. You make it another day. One day at a time. That's all you need to say to yourself every day. One day at a time. That's all you can do. That's how you make it in life. I'm a survivor. I enjoy life each day as much as I can. I'm not out to hurt anyone. I hated to stab that guy with my knife, but he, I thought, was wrong and he had a bad day. I feel good. I still was stabbed in the leg, but I also will mend. My dog is dead, but I'm still alive 'cuz of him. I'm thankful for that. I'm blessed that I had him in my life. That's all I can say about that, must move forward in life. I will be okay. I think I can get another piece of wood to put on the fire and be blessed.

I go and get more wood. I put it on the fire I have and have some more flames to enjoy. I think of my grandpa, and he was a good man. When times were tough he went fishing. He always said, "You have a hook and line, you will survive in life. You will not starve. You will make it another day." I never forgot that. I fish and I get full. I will try again tomorrow, get to wash more windows and maybe find some other food. Maybe I can find a good restaurant to have a cup of coffee in the morning. I hope it's a good day tomorrow. I will know after that day is done. I pull my hat over my head, and I go to sleep under the bridge and stars. Clear night out. I see the Big Dipper. Let's sleep.

Narrator moment: He got full after a day of good fishing. Washed some car windows and a car, made a little of money, and now he has a good fire and he is warm by it and goes to sleep hoping for a good day tomorrow. What a story, hey. I hope you enjoy it. There is more to tell in a bit. I need some food myself and a good nap. I will be back for more of the story. Have a good night. Let's close our eyes.

Good morning, my fellow friends, it's time for a new day. That's how fast it went, just a sentence away from the start of a new day. Let's get back to the story I like to tell. Here we go, my friends.

Wow, what a night I had while I slept. I dreamed that I was with my grandpa fishing. I guess I was thinking about him. I get up and I head back to town. I walk down the road past a few buildings. I come upon a few stoplights. There are a lot of buildings in this city and lots of gas stations. I come to a corner, and at the corner I see a restaurant. I want some coffee. I am going to go in, but I figure I should clean up first. I walk a little farther and come upon a firehall. I walk around the building and I see a faucet. I go to turn it on to see if any water comes out, and it does. I then wash my face off and my hands. I make it quick so nobody sees me. I know I need a bath. I will soon.

I head back to the restaurant. I decide to go in and sit down. It is a nice restaurant, kind of like a ma-and-pa place. Home cooking. I go in and boy, does it smell good in there. Somebody made homemade pie. Apple pie. I can smell the fresh apples. I want a piece of pie and coffee. I go in and sit down by the window in the corner. The waitress comes over and takes my order. "I want apple pie and a cup of coffee, please." She says, "No problem. I will get that for you." I sit there and I think about what I need to do for the day. I need to move on soon. It's a tough city to be in. I will ask her if there is a homeless shelter around. I hope she doesn't take me the wrong way when I ask her. She comes with my pie and coffee and I ask her.

She says, "Yes, there is. You need to go down about six blocks down this street out here," as she points out the window. "Then you need to go left four blocks, and it will be on your right. You go into the side, down and down the stairs. The rooms and showers are down there. They will feed you a meal for the day and give you a night to sleep. If there is room for the night. You need to get there soon as you can; they fill up fast."

"Well, thanks for your info. I appreciate it."

"It's no problem. I work over there. I help out with the homeless and their needs. I help make beds and serve food. You get there soon, okay? I don't want you on the street tonight, k?"

"Okay, I will go over there when I get out of here."

"What's your name?" she asks.

"My name is Tom, Tom Buddy. I need a shower and a good night's sleep."

"That's good. My name is Jasmin, like it says on my nametag. When a new guy or lady shows up here and asks where a shelter is, I direct them that way and I pay for their meal here. So your pie and coffee is on me, okay? I have a brother named Tom and I haven't seen him, yet I always wonder where he is. He someday will come around and see his family."

"Well, okay, I will go over to the shelter and get some food and a good night's sleep tonight, thanks."

I then get up and head out the door. It doesn't dawn on me right away, but then I think about it. Was that my sister that I haven't (illegible)?"

Maybe it was, and I don't know it yet. I wonder if she knows me at all. I don't know if she is there tonight. I will ask her a few questions about the parents and brothers.

I head to the corner of the street and go down the block and head farther about six blocks. It is a busy place and lots of people. I get a lot of looks. Maybe I smell bad. Maybe I look homeless. Maybe I don't bathe.

I don't know, I can't worry about it now. I'm heading to the shelter and getting cleaned up. I do need a good bed for the night. I hope she will be there tonight. I would like to talk to her for a bit. I head down the other street four blocks. I see the building and it doesn't look like a homeless shelter at all. It looks like a business building of some sort. It is a new building. Well, I will go to the side door and go in and head downstairs. I hope it's the right building. I go in and go down the steps and go through the doors. I see beds—lots of beds. I see where they have meals set up. Lots of tables in the back part of the room, they say "Men" and "Women" bathrooms. Must be where the showers are. I will just go in there and see if anyone is around here. I don't see anyone here. I sit at a table and wait. I don't see anyone for about thirty minutes. They do have a clock in there on the back wall. It is quiet in here. I hope I'm in the right place. I turn around and a couple comes in with a baby and comes and sits down at the table, and then a couple more come in. Then I see somebody come out of the bathrooms. They have a pail in their hand and some soap. I bet they work here. They come up to me and ask if I am here to stay the night. I say I am and I need a shower. She is a bigger woman. "I cleaned the showers up and the bathroom, and you can go inside and take a shower and clean up. Supper will be ready in an hour." I am glad to hear that. I am happy that I found Jasmin and she told me where to go. I am very excited to stay the night.

I head into the bathroom. I have to go after that pie I had. It ran right through me. I then strip down and climb into the shower. I clean up. I come out of the shower, and I find a new set of clothes on the chair by the shower and a couple of towels. I see a pair of new shoes and pants, a shirt, and a warm jacket, and believe or not a pair of underwear for me. I haven't worn underwear in about ten years. I feel high class. I put them on after the shower and pair of pants and a shirt and the jacket, and I do remember to take out my knife I had in my pocket of my pants. I even have a pair of shoes with both laces in them. That is too much.

They also give me a pair of warm gloves and a winter hat to have when it gets cold out. I put it all on and put the winter hat in my pocket of the jacket they gave me. I feel good. I hope I didn't take them from someone. I don't think I did. I think they left them for me. I go out of the bathroom and look and notice a lot more people showed up. They are in line for the showers. I notice the tables have baskets out on them. I go to the tables and wait for the meal. This place really fills up with people. Lots of families, lots of kids. There are more homeless people around here than you think. I guess I live alone. I stay where no one sees me. I stay alone. Now I see other people out by the tables, and they are putting stuff in the baskets. The baskets are full of food. You wouldn't think someone would give so much. I notice people coming out of the shower rooms. The bathrooms. They go to sit down at the tables. Some I notice leave the building. I notice some took a basket and left the building. I can't understand it. They can have a place to stay tonight, but they leave. Well, I guess it gives more people a chance to stay somewhere warm for the night. I like it. I think there will be more that come in to stay. Lots of beds, well, maybe about fifty beds or so. There must be about a hundred people in here. They come for the food. I notice in the back room, where they come out with the food. More people, I notice someone from earlier. It is Jasmin. The lady I saw at the restaurant.

She is helping out for the night. I have to go say hi. I want to thank her for this place to stay tonight. I hope she will talk to me for a bit. I hope before she leaves, I want to visit. I don't know what to say. I could be right about the sister thing, but I also could be wrong. I don't know unless I ask her. Well, I need my food.

I go up to the tables where the food is, and Jasmin is standing there with a smile on her face. She says to me, "I like it when I see people from the restaurant come here for more food and a good night's sleep. It sure makes me feel good. I like to help people in need out. I don't have it as rough as some. I don't have to work at the restaurant, but I do for the people to visit with. I like people. How are you, Tom? I'm glad to see you again. I know that you're going to be okay tonight. You will have a full belly and a warm place to stay for the night. Here's your basket. Enjoy it.. I was hoping you'd come; I wanted to talk to you tonight, is that okay, Tom?"

I say, "That will be great. I would like that if you did. Actually, I was hoping you wanted to talk to me."

"You go ahead and sit over there and eat."

When I say I am happy to do that, I then go over to the table and sit down and eat my food out of my basket. It is very good. They have some chicken, they have apples and oranges. They have some green beans. They have mashed potatoes, some gravy. What a meal. They also have a sandwich in a bag for later. It looks like ham and cheese. I will eat that later tonight. They also have some bottled water and some juice. What a treat. I eat and eat, I get full. I hope I can eat like this again soon. I need a nap in a bit. What a meal. I drink the water and juice. I hope to get more another night. I hope I get to talk to Jasmin. I like her; she is nice and very nice to others. That goes far in life when you're nice to others. She has a heart. That's good. I watch people get their baskets and sit and eat their contents. I see others take the baskets and head out the door. I think that is good, too. They do think of the other people that need a bed more. Like I said, lots of families here with kids; they need to be warm. A family of five are in here. They have a good shower and clothes to wear and food to eat and a bed to sleep in for the night, that is great. I will give up my bed for someone that needs it tonight. Right now I will sit and wait for Jasmin to talk to me. She is really busy with the people. Giving out food and cleaning the bathrooms and giving out clothes and towels. People are cleaned up thanks to Jasmin. Well, the others help, too. There are about four people working there to serve a hundred of us. That's a lot of work. They are busy.

The beds are getting full, and I need a bed or I won't have one for the night. I go over to a bed. I lie down on it and pull my hat over my eyes and take a nap. I am tired for the day. I hope to get to know Jasmin a bit. I got to find out about stuff with her. If she isn't my sister, then I must leave the city and head out. I hope to find her in my travels. I need to get to New York to see my brother. I need to move on soon. I think of that before I take my nap. I can sleep a bit and then I can get up and let someone else sleep for a bit. I nap for a bit.

I wake up and I am wondering if Jasmin is still here. I see her. She in the kitchen. I will get up and go sit at the tables and wait to talk to her. I get up and go over to the tables and sit down. She still is busy. She is cleaning up stuff. I notice that she looks out here and sees me. She will talk to me soon. I can just relax and wait for her. I do have all night, I'm not going anywhere. I don't have a train to catch. I will stick around a while.

I sit there at the tables, and a few come and sit by me with their kids and baskets. They eat and then they go over to the beds and lie down. I'm glad the kids get a place for the night to sleep. That's what it's all about. Let the kids have the beds to sleep in. I see that family stick together. The oldest kids give the bed to the youngest. I notice that it reminds me of when my older brother Red gave me a bed to sleep in and I saw him sleep in the chair. He was a good kid and let me sleep in the bed. He didn't have to do that for me, but he did. I like to keep to myself a lot. I don't like to talk to a lot of people. I have the "I don't trust you" attitude about me. I care but to a point I do. I believe a man should be able to take care of oneself when he needs to. I don't like beggars. They need to work to get their stuff. I'm only here 'cuz I want to talk to Jasmin, or I would have gone back to the bridge to sleep. I still can after I talk to her. I will see how it goes. My mind goes into a lot of directions. I worry myself a lot. I worry about my food, if I should eat it or save it. I worry about a fire for the night to stay warm. I worry about staying dry for the night. I worry about my brothers. I worry about my sister I haven't even met yet. I don't know what she looks like or if she is still alive. I hope so. I hope Jasmin is her. I hope she is, then I know she's okay, got a job and helps others out. She will be okay and then I can move forward. I worry 'cuz I don't know what she thinks of me. I might not be her brother, but I wonder if I am. I hope so. I will feel better if I do know if it's her. I can move on and know she's okay. I don't want anything from her, I just want to know if she's okay. I hope to see her. I could be wrong, and I have to move on in the morning if she is not here. I will then find her someday. See how I worry? I was told once, "You can't worry about the what-ifs. It doesn't do anyone any good. You can get very ill if you worry too much. You just got to move on and like life and what it brings to you."

I put my head down and close my eyes for a bit. Lots of thinking, and I get headaches. It's not funny. My thinking goes out of whack. I get paranoid a lot. I'm afraid no one likes me, and I worried like that for years. I don't worry as much about it anymore. I'm just likely to move on and try for another beautiful day. I want my mind at ease. I want to know that everyone I know is okay. I then have a good day. I do a lot of thinking. It can make me sick. I can get my hopes up and get shot down with the truth. It hurts.

I get nervous breakdowns. I don't like it. I get lots of shit in my mind and it's tough on it. I don't know what to do to have the time.

I have stuff on my mind, and I don't know what to say. I talk to my-self a lot. I argue with myself. I worry a lot. I always think someone is after me. I don't like it. I have an illness. I have manic depression. They call it bipolar. It has different levels. I have the middle of in the middle. I feel it's getting worse but don't know. I used to take pills for it, but since I've been on my own I don't anymore. I write a bit. I sleep a lot. I don't always eat. I don't drink alcohol. Well, that's a plus. I think I would be dead by now if I did. I need help, but I'm running away from it. I just travel with my mind. I go places. I don't stick around places for too long. I want to be left alone. I don't trust anyone anymore. I was having a bad day when I was young. I don't know what else to say. I like to travel. I like places where no one knows me. I only want to know a few. I must move on after talking to Jasmin. I don't want to harm her with my illness. It pisses people off when I don't know what to do when I have a breakdown. I need lots of rest. I take naps, but sometimes that's not enough. My mind goes forever, and I don't know if it will ever stop. I'm a busy man in my mind. I believe so, anyway. I hope I can have a friend someday that I can trust.

I hope it's Jasmin, but if not I must leave the city. If she is, I will stick around for a bit. I will wash car windows and shovel streets. I don't know what I will do, I just want to relax someday. I need a fire soon. Fires make me feel good and relaxed. I like the flames; they make me feel free. The flames are the way of life. Bust free of your feelings. Let it all out. I feel good after a good fire. I sleep good when I have a fire. I see the flame and it calms me down. I guess maybe I don't like the dark. I like to have some light. Light keeps me calm. I guess they make lights for people with mental illness. I saw one in a window at a store before. I didn't have any money on me, but it didn't matter. I have nowhere to plug it into, and I don't need it much if I have the sun to be in. Rainy days make me sad. I get depressed a lot. I'm okay. I think of a place that makes me happy.

I like to fish and fish do bite in the rain. They bite in the dark, too. I like to fish, it's relaxing, and to have a fire at night and fish, what a place to be. Night fishing with a flame. Awesome. It's fun. You can get fish and clean it up and cook it right away. Then relax afterward and take a nap after and think of good things (illegible)

I feel a tap on my shoulder. I turn around, and it is Jasmin.

"Hi," she says, "I got time to talk to you now, Tom."

"Okay," I say. "I would like that very much."

"How are you doing?" she asks.

"I'm okay, a little tired but I'm okay. I've been doing a lot of thinking, and my mind gets tired."

"Yeah, I understand that. It happens to me. I get around people and I feel better. I like sunny days and good fishing."

"You like to fish?"

"Yeah, I like to fish. My dad would take me and my brother. I loved it. It sure helps the day go by and no worries."

"I like to hear that," I say. "You said you have a brother?"

"Yeah, I have a brother, Tom. He is my twin brother. I don't know where he is right now. He went off to school in March and he hasn't talked to anyone in a long time. I wish he would call us soon."

"You have a twin brother named Tom?"

"Yeah, my mom had us at sixteen years old. Then she died after giving birth to us."

"What was her name?"

"It was Trisha."

"You have other family members?"

"Yes, I came from a bigger family. I have four uncles, and my dad is still around. I see him now and then. We don't talk much. He didn't like the thought of me waitressing in such an area, that I shouldn't be around people that need food and a bed. I told him I like what I do and I don't need to be told different. He got mad and told me to find a place to live then and go. So I found a place down the road from here and I love what I do, for now, anyway."

"Who are your uncles?"

"Well, one of them is a boxer and the other two work, and I think the other one is somewhere in the country. He hasn't gotten ahold of anyone. He left on his own when he was seventeen years old and hasn't talked to anyone. I would love to meet him someday. Mom talked about him. She said that he has an illness of some sort. I wish I would help him if he was 'round to help. I always like to help people and special someones in the family. I think he needs family now. I know he does."

"Can I ask you a question? How old are you?"

"I'm twenty-eight years old."

"You're eighteen years old and you're on your own?"

"Yep, I live all alone."

"Well, I haven't met my sister ever. She was ten years younger than me, I mean. I didn't know her name or anything. I've been looking for my family for a long time. I'm lost. I live day by day to find them all. My name is Tom Buddy. Was your name Buddy?"

"Yes, I am a Buddy. Mom never married, so yes, I'm after her last name. She named my brother after her brother that she was hoping to meet someday, but she never got the chance to."

"Well, I'm Tom Buddy and I think I'm your uncle. My brothers are Darrel (illegible).

I found out Randel became a boxer and Darrel owns a gas station in Seattle."

"Yes, that's true. Well, I'm glad to know you, Tom. Mom is looking down and putting us together, I believe. My grandfather was put in prison, and so was my grandma, for drugs."

"Yes, I left. I couldn't handle it all. I needed to leave. I am so happy to find you."

"Tom, let's go to my place and talk some more, okay?"

"Okay, we can, Jasmin."

I wake up with the sound of a freight train going over the bridge. I was sleeping. I thought I was awake but I wasn't; I had a dream. I feel the rumble of the train under the bridge. The dream felt real, like it happened and I was with a gal named Jasmin. I really thought she was my sister that I hadn't ever met. It was her daughter and she had died. What a dream. I hope it is okay. I hope to still meet my sister somewhere. I hope she's okay. I would love to meet her someday. I must be getting close to family if I'm dreaming of them a lot. I hope they are okay. I need to find them soon. I need to move on toward New York. I got to see my brother Red in a fight. I will plan to leave in a bit. I hope I can get back on a train that goes to Chicago. I got to get back toward the railyard. I will find the right train to Chicago. I need to leave tonight.

It is getting dark out, and I need to go to the railyard to get on a train. I head toward the railyard, where I came off the train before. I cross over the one hundred tracks and look toward the east and I look toward the west. I don't see any trains yet. I wait, thinking about my dream. I hope my sister is okay. I should find out soon. I hope she could be in Chicago, but I don't know about that either. I look up and I see a headlight in the distance that is heading toward me, going east. That's the one, I hope. Let's see if it is. I step back a few steps and watch the train as it gets closer. It is a big train and big engines. It must be the one I need. I then let it get closer, and it goes by me and it is slowing down a bit. It has a few boxcars coming up. I need to be a little farther down so they don't see me. I wait and about half a mile I notice a few tank cars and then I see a few box-cars. I wait for it to stop and it does, and I get up to go see the cars. I then run a bit to get to the boxcars. I come up to the boxcar and the door is cracked open a bit, and I am able to climb into it. I get in there and I go behind some crates. I sit down for a bit and wait for the train to go and get past the depot. I don't want to be seen. I need to get to Chicago. I hope this one takes me there. I get my breath and

I feel the train moving, and I am on the train in a boxcar. I am on the move again. I am nervous about it. I am scared, actually, because the dream felt real. I need to find out who she is someday. I hope I do. I go by the depot in the boxcar.

I am on my way to New York. I'm glad to be leaving Seattle. I hope to find my family. I think I should start looking them up on my way to New York. My oldest brother Darrel, he works everywhere, does anything. I don't know where I should start looking for him. I will figure it all out when I get going. I like the fact that I am heading to New York, such a big world out there. I hope my dreams come true. I hope to find them.

Narrator moment: I guess I had you going on the dream he had, hey. I hope you're still interested to know what's coming ahead in this trip of his. He is on his way to find his family. He has been on the lookout for them for years. He takes the train across the countryside to find them, and you need to keep following the story. Dreams are real if you believe in them. Let's get back to the story. He gets on the train in Seattle, and he needs to get to New York. Well, I hope he gets there. What a start. Here we go now.

I am sitting in the boxcar behind some crates. I am hearing a whine. I look up and there is a dog just like in my dream. It is a yellow lab. I can't believe it. It's like I've already been here. I'm now with a dog, and it's the beginning of a good trip so far. Boxcar, it's got to be Boxcar. He comes up to me and licks my face. He sits beside me. I like it now. Let's not get into trouble this time.

We ride the train from Seattle to Fargo, and we stop outside of the city. We grab some corn and we are back on our way on the train. We go to St. Paul through the twin cities, and we stop outside of the St. Paul area. We get out for a bit, and we are checking out the area. It is weird that I have a dog that was in my dream and we are together again but never were before, only in a dream. Well, I will keep him as long as I can. We will keep him on the train until we at least get to

Chicago. We do get back on the train, and we are on the move again. We are going along the St. Croix River. What a view to see. It's hard to explain but to see it. Bluffs behind and the river in front, the sun is shining, it's a cool day. We have gone by Hastings and coming up to Red Wing. I want to see more of the river, maybe later. I am thinking about my past and I don't like what is happening to the train at the moment. It is shaking back and forth, side to side, it's getting really rough. We are out of control and we are nervous. The train is derailed and we are off the track and in the ditch. We are on our side and we slam against the wall of the boxcar. That hurt. I sit straight up.

I wake up from a dream. I am on a couch. My niece gives me a blanket and puts it on me. I am sweaty. I don't feel good at the moment. I am shook up. I look at the wall, and it has a clock on it. It reads "12:30 A.M." It has to be midnight or after, I guess. I think of Boxcar a bit. We had a derailment. I was hurt and Boxcar was okay. Well, I must move on with my sleeping. I do need to get back on the train and head out of town. I need some more sleep. I will leave in the morning. I have to go, I know I do. It will be okay.

Narrator moment: What a dream he had. Well, I think we need to get back to the story now and see what happens in the morning. I hope you're enjoying this.

The light coming through the shade of the window wakes me up. It is morning. My niece isn't up yet, but I know I need to go. Then I hear a noise coming down the hallway. My niece is up and she says, "Hi, good morning, Tom. How was your sleep?"

"I slept okay, but I do need to get going."

"You can hang out here for a bit. I don't have to work until 1 P.M. today."

"Okay. I do need to go soon."

"Okay."

"Thanks for the couch to sleep on. It's been a long time that I slept on a couch."

"You're welcome. Do you want some coffee?"

"Yes, that would be great."

She gets my coffee and I take a sip.

"Tom, I need to know more about you. I heard story after about you, but I'm glad to have met you."

"I don't have much to talk about. I left on my own when I was seventeen. I found odd jobs and rode the rails. I keep quiet about my life to anyone. I don't like to talk about much. I am a survivor. I live day by day. I like my freedom. I like to go fishing. I fish to survive now. I like it. I like to ride the rails. I had a dog but he died. I had to bury him down by the riverbank. I met you. You brought me here to sleep. I thank you for that. What else do you need to know?"

"I want to know if you want to know where any of your family are."

"I don't know if I'm ready for that. I like to live my life and not interfere with them. I don't want anything from them. I just want to live my life. I do want to know one thing, though. Do you know where Danniel is?"

"I do. He had lived in Chicago, and he works for the newspaper out there. He got married and has a couple of kids. They now live in New York, the kids do, and Danniel lives still in Chicago."

"I would love to see him sometime. Do you know where he lives over there?"

"I do. He lives on Park Street. I don't have his full address, but he lives by a water park. That's all I know."

"I would like to stop in and see him sometime."

"I think that would be cool if you did. He got good kids. I like them. Why don't you stick around and tell me about yourself? I would love to get to know you a little bit."

"Well, okay, what do you want to know?"

"Were you ever married?"

"No, I wasn't."

"Do you have any kids out there?"

"No, not that I know of."

"Where did you live with your brothers?"

"We were from Minnesota. The northern area. Cold in the winters. Beautiful in the summer and fall."

"I wondered that because my mother didn't live with you guys."

"No, she was not born yet. I left with my aunt and uncle when I was nine. We moved around a lot. We were in the southern area. Florida. I left them when I was seventeen. I left 'cuz I figured I was a burden on them. I needed to live life without any family. I liked it at the time. I did what I wanted to do. I worked when I wanted to and I slept wherever. I worked lots of jobs. I didn't stick around much at those jobs, but I learned a lot. I have my issues, and I didn't want anyone to know about me. I wanted to be left alone. I'm a good man. I just like it that I can do my own living."

"Where were you from?"

"I was from here also. I grew up with Dad and brother. We lived here in the twin cities, and I don't want to leave if I can help it."

"What put you on the street, though, Tom?"

"I didn't want to be around people much. I like to keep quiet. I've been on the streets my whole adult life. I tried to get good jobs, but I had bad reading skills. I was not good with numbers or words. I could write but not that great. I like to travel around, see different things out there. I like the view of mountains. I like the view of the ocean. I like to fish. I like fires. My health is not bad. It could be better, but it is what it is. I need to work on people skills a little. I have a hard time among people. Large amounts of people. I worry about what they would think of me. I worry about everything. I have to work on that. I like one-on-one. I have a hard time when it's more than two. I always feel like the third wheel. I get nervous. I don't think I'm important. I feel ashamed with myself a lot. I get worked up about it. I have lots of breakdowns in my mind. It's no fun. I don't ever want to hurt anyone. I want to figure it out on my own. I had a dog that traveled with me, but he died. I came to the cities here a couple of days ago. I loved him. I could tell him everything and anything. He loved me, too. He saved my life, and I thank him for that but I wish he was with me still. I miss him. His name was Boxcar. I found him in a boxcar on my way here, and I was hoping he would still be with me. I run away a lot with my problems. I do run. I want to forget it all, but I have a hard time with it."

"What is it you're wanting to forget?"

There is a knock at the door. I am glad because I'm not ready to tell my story about that. She goes to the door and opens it, and her friend comes in.

"This is my Uncle Tom."

"How are you?"

"I'm fine."

I tell Jasmin that I am going to leave and come back later.

"Okay, I will see you later."

I get out of there. I go down the street. I head to the city. I want to leave on the next train. I said I would go back there, but I don't want to talk anymore about my life. I'm not ready for that. I don't like my past—most of it, anyway. I come to a bench on a corner. I decide to sit there for a bit. I take a seat and I am thinking about it all. I am worked up about it. I don't like it. I want to leave the area. I know I have to go back and visit with her. I will, I guess. I do think she's okay. I don't have to talk about it if I don't want to. My mind is full right now. I need a fire and to do some fishing.

I get up and head toward the river bridge. I need to do some cat fishing. I need to clear my mind. I'm hungry, too. I want to be able to relax with my thoughts. There are a lot of people downtown. They look at me with disgust. I don't look the best or smell the best right now. I should have showered at her place. I will when I go back. I'm sitting under the train bridge with my line in the water, fishing for the big cats. Now I'm relaxed. I need to get the fire going in a bit. I stick the end of the rod in the mud. I get up and start to look for some firewood. I get many arms full. I get some leaves and bark. I still have a match left in my book of matches. I get it ready to light, and I light up the fire. I get the fire going and a few sticks get a good flame. I can now relax with my thoughts. I grab my fishing rod. I check the line, worm still on hook. I cast it back in the water. I am fishing with a flame. What a combo. I should leave on the next train, but I will stick around and talk to her. I need to get to know my niece. Find out about her mother, my sister. I wonder if she got a picture of her for me. I never knew what she looked like. I wonder if she looks like me. I will find out. It's been a while since I looked in the mirror at myself. No, I looked in the mirror the other day and I'm getting older as we speak. I'm old, I'm laughing at myself. I am older, but I'm wiser than I was when I was young. I wish I could have a better young life. It was the way it went. You appreciate more in life when it is tough. I think everyone should have some tough times. You really do feel good when good stuff happens to you. I'm glad I met up with my niece. She is a good kid. I believe she was probably like her mother. I'm glad we found each other. I can get to know her and the rest of the family in time. She can tell me a lot about the family if she talks to them.

I now have a bite. It's a nibble now. It's pulling my line down. It's a big bite. I set the hook. I am reeling in, it's a fighter. It's pulling, I'm still reeling in. I get up to the top and reel it into the shore. It's another cat, about eight pounds. That's good food. I have a fire and am ready to cook. I gut it out. I do have a stick to put it on and over the fire. I am cooking cat on the fire. What a meal to have. I turn it and the oil is coming out of it now, and it's time to eat. I take it off the stick and peel the skin back, and there is the meat. It's white, flaky meat, beautiful food. Thanks for the meal, God. I bite into it. Yum, it's good. I eat until I am full. I see an old pan behind me. I put some water into it. I put on the fire. I boil the water and then let it sit. It cools down and I drink it. Good water, now I feel good. Time for a nap. I pull my hat down over my eyes and goodnight, my friends.

Narrator moment: Okay, you have three cats fighting among each other. Then they are licking each other for five minutes. I thought to share that moment with you. Okay, let's see, we had Tom see his niece at her place, then a friend stopped over and Tom left for a bit. Tom then went fishing and got one, and he had a fire and ate it up. He was full and took a nap. My cats did the same thing. They ate and took a nap. Okay, we are ready now. Let's see, I got my coffee and I'm ready to tell the story again. Here we go.

The sound of a train wakes me up. I'm up now. I get up and head back to my niece's place. I hope she is there, yet she said she had to work at one. I don't have a watch, but it might be noon the way the sun is. I get into the city, and on the bank wall there is a clock and it says "12:15 P.M." I am getting closer to her home. It's an apartment, a small home, and it's a nice place. Well, I think she is home. I go to the door and knock on it. She is home and she lets me in.

"How are you, Tom? My friend left a bit ago, and I was wondering if you were going to stop by again. I was hoping you were. What were you up to?"

"I did some fishin' and ate a catfish. It was yummy."

"I would love to go fishin' sometime."

"I will keep that in mind next time, we will go."

"I have to get ready to go to work. You are welcome to stay here until I get home from work today."

"Okay, I will. Do you have any pictures of your mother that I can see and have?"

"I do, and I will get them out when I get home today, okay?"

"Okay. I will be looking forward to seeing them when you get home."

She gets herself ready for work and heads out the door. I am looking at the clock and notice it is 12:45 P.M. She has to be at work at 1. She will make it. I sit on the couch. I turn the TV on and watch a little bit of it. I start to think about my young years. I watched some TV when I was a kid but not much. We went outside and played more often. I am okay with the TV on for a bit. I watch some news that is on. It talks about all the bad stuff that goes on out there. I try to stay away from that kind of stuff. I don't want any part of it. I like to stay by myself. I like to do stuff alone. I like to stay alone and sleep alone. I like to know I'm my own man. I don't have to take care of anyone. I just take care of myself. I like it that way.

I get up off the couch and go to the refrigerator and open it and see some leftover chicken she has, so I eat that. I see some milk in there and I drink that. I see some cookies on the counter and I eat some. It was all good. I lie down on the couch and I take a nap. I feel like I am in heaven with the couch and all the food to eat. The TV is on. I am comfortable. It feels like home for a moment. I am thinking of my niece and I hope she is having a good day at work. I'm proud of her to have a job and her own place to live. I have to just wait for her to come home to see some pictures of her mother, my sister. I haven't never seen them. I wonder if she looks like me. I wish that I saw her, but it is what it is. I then close my eyes and fall asleep.

I open my eyes, and I am in a grass field. There is a train in the distance. I turn around and there is an image of a lady reaching out to me. I am nervous but not afraid. I feel comfort. I am thinking like a kid. I am about five years old, and it looks like my mother, and I am going to run toward her. I then run the other way and go toward the train. I run through the field of grass. I go up to the train to get on it and the train speeds up. I can't get on it; it is too fast for me. I turn around and the lady is still there with her hand out for me to grab. I go toward her, and behind me the train goes off the track, lots of cars pile up. It is a big pileup. What a derailment. The lady is still there and I run toward her and I wake up.

I look at the wall in front of me, and there is the clock again. It reads "4:00 P.M." I wonder if my niece will be home soon. I guess she might work until eight or nine. I don't know. I had a weird dream. I remember that I had another train derailment dream. I don't know why I'm having those. That lady image was pretty and it wasn't my mother. I don't know who it was. I am weirded out by it. I really wonder who it was in my dream. I will figure it out someday. I need to find something else to do.

I notice on the coffee table there is a book. It says: "Dreams and Where They Come From." I pick it up and look through it. I am curious about it. I open and read a little. I see in there about why your mind travels around like that. I don't understand what it means, so I put it down. I don't remember much about it. I don't read too good, so I don't get into it. I can write okay but not much for reading words. I don't always understand what I read. So I don't read much. I look at the clock and it reads "6 P.M." Well, maybe she will be home soon. I turn the TV on for a bit longer and see what is on. Lots of news. Weather I don't care much about. I'm just wasting time. I don't know what to do until she gets home. I could leave for a bit, but if she comes home and I'm not here she will think I left her. I will just sit here and wait. I just have to leave on that train tonight and get out of town. I need to feel free again. I feel trapped here. I think people are after me. I'm paranoid. I hate when I feel this way. It really brings me down. I can't think right, and I don't eat. I have no fun with this. I need to leave and go. I said I would stay, but I can't. I got to leave this city now. The world is falling into me. I can't hold it up anymore. I need to calm down, and I need to count backward for a bit. "1000, 999, 998, 997, 996, 995, 994, 993, 992, 991, 990." Okay, I can think a little better now. Okay, I will wait here for her to come back to me. I got to talk to her about her mother. My sister. I need to see what she looks like. She should be home soon.

I turn the TV back on. I turn it to a channel that has birds on it. I start to relax a bit. It comes and goes. My mind goes a hundred miles an hour and then in overdrive and then the brakes go on till it stops. Fast and out-of-control thinking. I used to take meds but don't anymore. I just run from problems. Listen to birds. Maybe write stuff down. It's all good to do. I need to calm down my thinking. I can only handle so much at one time. I have slow thinking, maybe put too fast to comprehend what I'm sayin'. I think I should leave now. My leg hurts from the stabbing. I have to clean it up.

I then go into the bathroom and find some bandages and alcohol to rub on it. It really hurts. I find some bandages and some alcohol to rub on my wound. I pour it on my leg and clean it up and put another bandage on it. I find some med tape and put that on it to hold it on there. I go out into the living room. I go to sit down on the couch for a bit. There is a knock at the door. I don't know anyone and no one knows me. I don't want to answer it, but it could be my niece with her arms full on stuff. I can open the door, I guess; she knows I'm here.

I get to the door to open it up. I then open the door. It is an older lady and a couple of guys. I don't know them and I would like to let them in, but it's not my place so I say, "Jasmin is not here. Can I help you? I'm her Uncle Tom."

They come in, and then they go to shake my hand, I think. They reach out and pull my arm back behind my back. I am up against the wall then, and they put my hands in cuffs. I don't know what's going on here.

"I have a right to be here. I know Jasmin; she's my niece."

"You are coming with us."

"You don't understand me. I know Jasmin, my niece."

"We know you have a niece, but she's not here."

"This is her place, and I'm visiting her."

"It's not her place, and you need to come with us, Tom."

"How you know me? I don't know you guys."

"You know me through the glass."

"What glass?"

"I'm your doctor."

"Doctor who? I don't have a doctor. I live on my own, and I'm on my own, man. I need to go to New York. I need my family."

"You will be with your family. You need our help."

"I need to be in New York to see my brother, and I need to find my other brother in Chicago. I don't know what you are doing to me, let me go."

I'm fighting to get away from them. They put me on the ground, and they give me a shot in the ass.

"You will start to feel better in a bit."

I don't know what is going on, then I fall asleep, get drowsy. I slur my words. I close my eyes. I last saw my niece when she came into the room. I don't know anymore. I'm worried about her. I left her. They took me. I don't know anyone, where am I? It's dark and I'm afraid. I don't like the dark. Where am I? The lights are out. I need some light, where am I? Please, someone tell me where I am. I don't see no one. I am lost, where is my sister then? I thought I was going to see her picture. I am in a dream, aren't I? I just haven't woken up yet. I need to wake up. Please wake me. I'm scared, don't leave me like this. I didn't mean to do it. I don't know who did. I think I need my dog. I miss my dog, Boxcar. Please, please, talk to me, someone.

The light comes on, and I'm in some room. It has some kind of padding on it. A padded door with a little window to see out of it. What's going on here? Am I back where I was when I was eighteen years old? I left this place. I left to be on my own. I'm my own person. I have a good mind. I've left this place. Why am I here? I don't understand. I'm talking and I'm walking, why am I doing that? I'd love to know why I'm in here. In this padded room. I go to the window to look out. There is a man at the door.

I say to him, "Who are you and what am I doing here?"

"Well, hello, Tom. It's nice to hear from you, it's been a while. I will get the nurses. They want to talk to you."

"Why am I here?"

"They'll let you know what you want to know. Relax, Tom, you're going to be okay."

The nurses come into the room and want to talk to me.

"I want to know why I'm in here."

"You just have woken up from a mental stroke to your brain. You're at a hospital to get some help, and you have just woken up and we put you in here just for now. I want to explain to you what happened. Let's get you out of this room and put you in another one. We'll get you out."

We go to another room down the hall. The hallway has a few windows to some rooms. There is a desk and a few nurses are at it. There is a ater fountain. They bring me into this light room with some windows in it that look outside. There are some trees out there and a waterfall, a pond-looking thing. They bring me to a chair to sit down. So I sit in the chair and the lady sits across from me. I have no idea who this gal is.

"I'm your sister, Tom. I'm a doctor here at this hospital. I'm here to help you."

"What? I lost my sister; she died giving birth."

"Nope, that's what is in your mind. I'm Trisha. I do have a daughter named Jasmin. I called her first when you came to."

"What? I was at her place."

"No, Tom, you were here. You had a breakdown with your mind, and it shut you down. So your mind did some traveling while you were here."

"Well, do I get out then?"

"We have to do more tests first."

"What tests do you have to do?"

"Got to check on your brainwaves. I want this to work out for you and our family. You need to be on your pills again, and you will come around a bit later. I am here to watch over you. You will be okay, Tom. You don't remember me, do you? I was a little girl when we met. You did live with our aunt and uncle. I came and saw you. We played a lot together. You dreamt of me 'cuz you remember me. I am in your thoughts 'cause I am working with you to get you better."

"My trip on the train felt real."

"You used to work on the railroad. You liked the railroad. You liked to ride trains. You liked to travel. Your mind was on the job."

"I had a dog in my thoughts."

"Yes, you had a dog when you were young."

"In my thoughts his name was Boxcar."

"Yes, your dog's name was Boxcar."

"In my thoughts I had my brothers."

"Yes, you have three brothers."

"Their names were Darrel, Randel, and Danniel."

"Yes, you have your brothers' names right, but one has died."

"Who died?"

"Randel. He was killed in a fight with a bunch of guys on the street. He was murdered."

"No, not Red."

"Yes, he was."

"I was going out to New York to watch him fight."

"Yes, but he was killed in the streets of New York."

"He was a fighter."

"No, that's what you thought of him. He hung out on the streets and didn't have a job. He got himself into trouble with the law. He was murdered after he was out of the jail."

"No, he was my brother that took care of me when I needed him."

"When you were young, yes."

"How long was I out?"

"You have been out for one year. You went into a coma. You have been in here for five years. We've been taking care of you. You had a mental breakdown. Lots of stress. I was here to help you. My daughter came to see you for that year. She wasn't giving up on you."

"Jasmin?"

"Right, yes, Jasmin."

"If I'm going to be okay, am I able to go home yet?"

"Well, I don't think so. For now you have to stay in here."

"Where is here?"

"In the State hospital. You're getting help and you have come a long way. We've worked on you for a while now, and you need to stay here."

"I want my life back."

"You will have your chance to."

"I do want to know one thing. I had an image of a woman in my thoughts. She was reaching out to me and I woke up. Who was that woman in my mind?"

"I don't know, we can work with it."

"What was her name? I need to know who she was. Do you have an answer for me? Who pulled me out of the dream?"

"You had a lot on your mind, didn't you, Tom?"

"Who was she? Where'd she go? Is she here? What's her name?"

Narrator moment: Who was the lady that pulled him out of the mind? I hope you all enjoy the story. For this time around. Tom came out of his coma, and who was she? Find out in the next read.